SONG & GLASS STAN MIR

Subito Press • Boulder, Colorado • 2010

Subito Press is a nonprofit literary publisher based in the Creative Writing Program of the Department of English at the University of Colorado at Boulder. We look for innovative fiction and poetry that at once reflects and informs the contemporary human condition, and we promote new literary voices as well as work from previously published writers. Subito Press encourages and supports work that challenges already-accepted literary modes and devices.

2009 Competition Winners

Fiction: Tracy DeBrincat, *Moon is Cotton & She Laugh All Night*
Poetry: Stan Mir, *Song & Glass*

Subito Press
Boulder, Colorado
www.subitopress.org

Library of Congress Cataloging in Publication
Data available upon request

978-0-9801098-7-0

Generous funding for this publication has
been provided through an Innovative Seed
Grant from the University of Colorado at
Boulder, and by that university's Creative
Writing Program.

Contents

for Michael Gizzi

OPPOSITE OF AUTUMN

The faces in the windows
are not petals of a flower

nor those of a bicycle
they are faces paddling

through an afternoon
offset by geometry that

measures what shape
we're in rather than the

shape we should be

stripped free of bone
I could be

malleable to anyone's
wish a good

samaritan to the
individual who

bends me every which
way everything is

permitted & not negotiable
according to the

terms agreed upon
b/w my fiscal

master & me I will
take & I will

go where no spine
needs a home

live w/ no accord
as I must I see

no way
towards truth

yet this state is
mostly sea

a guest in a house
a house in a guest

the door through the wall
the wall through the door

if what we want is
not so then we make

what we want so we have
what we need what we need

is a window toward light
toward light I move

like light able to
refract & aberrate

for worth I make
want resemble need

put glass in its eyes
ask it speak on matter

in a dark space on matter
speak how we see

through glass through glass
walls we see what we see

30 days near gone sun still
reports through the air what

matters to be seen in the
hallway's reflections rippling

along the floor where at
its end a door is ajar a

partial chair seen then more
light through glass & leaves

or is it leaves then glass
seen out in the air what

I meant was or is it leaves
then light seen out in air

does distance determine boundary
where none may be discerned

who's to say any line
holds exactitude hostage

stretching out the line always
does what it's meant to

that is connect what is
already connected by

similar existence by
virtue of placement

here on earth where most
see what takes place

if not then sight trans-
poses itself to another

sense like feeling my
skin burns in light & I

feel that I love what's
past to want more to pass

I just wrote what came
because it was all put here

experience rises up like
stones on a wall &

our will to stand grows
more determined

like a boundary between
what can & cannot be done

good deal gone

bad

we

speak

the same

as those

who

ate burgers

& fries

10 yrs ago

language as spoken

distorts

the seen

into

truth

maybe

not

the truth is

in what

structure puts

forth

          an edifice

erected

        is a form

                    starting

over

          not from

                scratch its

ground wire

                  protects us

          from pain

                    caused

by error

out the window

autumnal

guides

an insect crawls

towards

a glass of water

if only

surroundings' details would become

significant

this wish   something

most

wish

for there are too many

voices

perhaps

since it is

sound   partially

that

attracts us

to

poetry

vision

attracts

certainly

our heads

are kept

down too often

if one could perfect looking

up while

writing

between the lines

then

details would rise

like edifices

on a horizon

scuffed

by presence

It is not yet winter it is
already cold
enough to create
snow drifts in the mind.

The house we thought
we lived in was
sold. Its agent gorged
on dimes in the

imaginary beehive's
shadow. This sounds
like dream. Her face was
printed as if marked

by a mint. Her mediocre
head in a back-
ground of green. Significant
activity takes place

daily. Real Estate is
not much more
than a fishbowl
polluted. It wants more

shit before it lets you breathe.

The din comes as rain I am
a person of weather locked in a parade
what was halcyon is gone the tuba
honks flat as if a wall
collapsed inside.

Once I tried to place
a choir in a boy's larynx
the task proved viral from the
beginning it should've
been simple to incise

his throat he would thus be
polyvocal & no more alone
than before each voice broke into
one which botched my idea
he could travel without reaching

for song. The din always
comes wrong we listen to its
dull hum never intending
to listen long & end up
hissing in the form of accompaniment.

The din comes as sun
shadow across the face
as I carry these several
things I would not

name but do: Marantz
cassette recorder, books
by Koeneke, Johnson, &
Heliczer. I'm not sure

what colors are safe
to say represent emotion.
Shadow takes
day drubs it into being

dawn drubs me
into the shards I
recognize from
the night before.

"Arguably a cicada,
  folding its wings into hymns"
goes within for its song.
I'd do right by this

as long as I get purchase
on what comes in as din.

The will is a forlorn god who began as a wave at sea
forgotten in the scheme of determinations
put forth by a vision of the bird mid-flight.

To sweep the skies at will kill all delusions
of grandeur for the sake of modesty. If
I were to take any of this seriously I'd be

seismic in my faults. The will was never a god.
It was what it is now. A name for what we try
to force upon ourselves in the shadow of others.

I will never truly be funny unless pressed to be
clairvoyant in the company of my heroes as they
think of ways to be rid of me & my will.

I drink this pink bismuth
each morning – my gut
rots the fallen walnuts
in the yard – rain follows
rain as my wait for baseball's
game continues – Caro-
line calls brings more
Narragansett – this could
be the late 1970s
it's 2005 what a fine
name for a year James
Schuyler once said
about 1968 – Caroline
said Schuyler removes
all cant from contemporary
poetry – to me she says
I can't stand those who
dislike art – it takes shapes
for things to fit – try to
stop comparing myself
to others – would money
solve our problems – pay
our debts – so we'd have
the rhino of our dreams

They call this civil
engineering this block

building adheres to
the sky a thumb

a genie couldn't
change this

a wrecking ball
could repeatedly

slam this brutality
into slabs with which

we could sculpt mon-
uments to surveillance

I spy taste exists
on one's tongue

we need it in our
eyes what is

ugly is ugly & must
not change what is

beautiful exists
look to the margins

where things remain
unharmed lions

in the bush what
do we do when these

lions enrage our sensibility
& turn what is brutal

into what is beautiful

Forever dedicated to the
opposite of autumn these
leaves fathom their errors
with the expertise of
girls clamoring up the
stairs to a building
called daylight abstraction
has become commonplace
in a world of imagined things
one's objective is clear
to sit on a bench & stare
at pacifists on bicycles
failure kicks about on
a plateau shadow relieves
itself of duty due to diminished
use like ideals shadow
never had an actual economy
overabundant cadavered
upright dolls we choke
the mediocre walks up
the street a tarnish in its
eye proclaims our chances
dead or at least slim to
none no more tight syntax
futile like twins basking
in the sun for a game to be
what its worth it must have
an architecture of note

A blitzkrieg on your house you scorch
monkey like a chalkboard you've
been declared dirty you continually
smudge my song when concentration's
at its worst I think this bomb's
got a chance to kill you can be replaced
others have been by bullets or sickness
I ain't got much time the phone's
tapped who could assassinate what
can't be seen Banks McGillicudy
the champeen of the mundane
declares the obsolete a hero he says
lies never go out of style the idealist
lies continually to himself & others
a job away from assholes doesn't exist
the imagination is capable of anything
except reality break my face get gone
the stars are telling the truth things
fade and sometimes burst it was long ago
but I heard space isn't what it used to be

grey

against a grey sky

juxtapose syntax

                          while eating a burger

      in an alley

               you'll look

         like a scoundrel   slipping

on wrappers

               in a remote region

of the Andes

           a condor is tied

                    to the back of a bull

they

struggle

                    until released

     the condor

        turns

             freedom into an exercise

      Harriet Miers

            recoils

                    no bridge from Texas

         to wherever she planned

                              to go

her face lampooned

            perpetually

                     matches nothing

I live in this small city the world teems with
possibility. Engines rise. Water.

Elements hold sway. Mid-autumn sun
gambles. The textile mill turns what's past wool.

Where children walk confetti screams invisibility.
Candy. Ornate wish engraved upon a sidewalk:

BUILT BY WORKS PROGRESS ADMINISTRATION
1935-1937. Garbage cans have been chucked.

The breeze takes them like larger men. Tosses them.
Change within pattern emboldens pattern.

One stone demolishes another stone. Where
we end up is never where we began.

No dictation comes
to take me
away the rain
slants into
windows gales
dictate day's
discourse
a hard agenda

Subject to anatomy's
faults as if a house
whose foundation
cracked & roof
rotted time lapses

Why is the time
before one's
birth not also
considered death

This bench has ceased
comfort in the sun

the tape rewinds the birds
an ant carrying a leaf

fleck crawls circuitously
I have folded

my notebook due to wind
the tape rewinds Joe

Ceravolo who died September
4, 1988 while I turned

12 girls told me my voice
changed the phone just

rang I am headed to New
York once again all

I think is certain slants
of sunlight tell more faults

the tape has rewound
what I haven't yet

heard is who will take
what I offer when I

offer it will I fall
on my knees

then   will
I lift what has already

lifted what the tree said
lifted into this poem

good fortune rings
but twice a man sits

across the park the breeze
across the park the asshole

walks across the park the wind
lifts my notebook pages

I imagine the light Californian
should I listen to the tape

or hold it to imagine what
it says I want to write a poem

to my friends Andy & Jed
                    I want them

to know I will never stop giving
someone told me so it is Friday

November 4 President Bush
pushes his course in Latin America

I think it's time for the tape:
press play

Denby, the light, or is it the clouds,
above the bridges in America.
Time fades into the girders.

It is hard to get anything done
when the mind holds
aspirations outside reality.

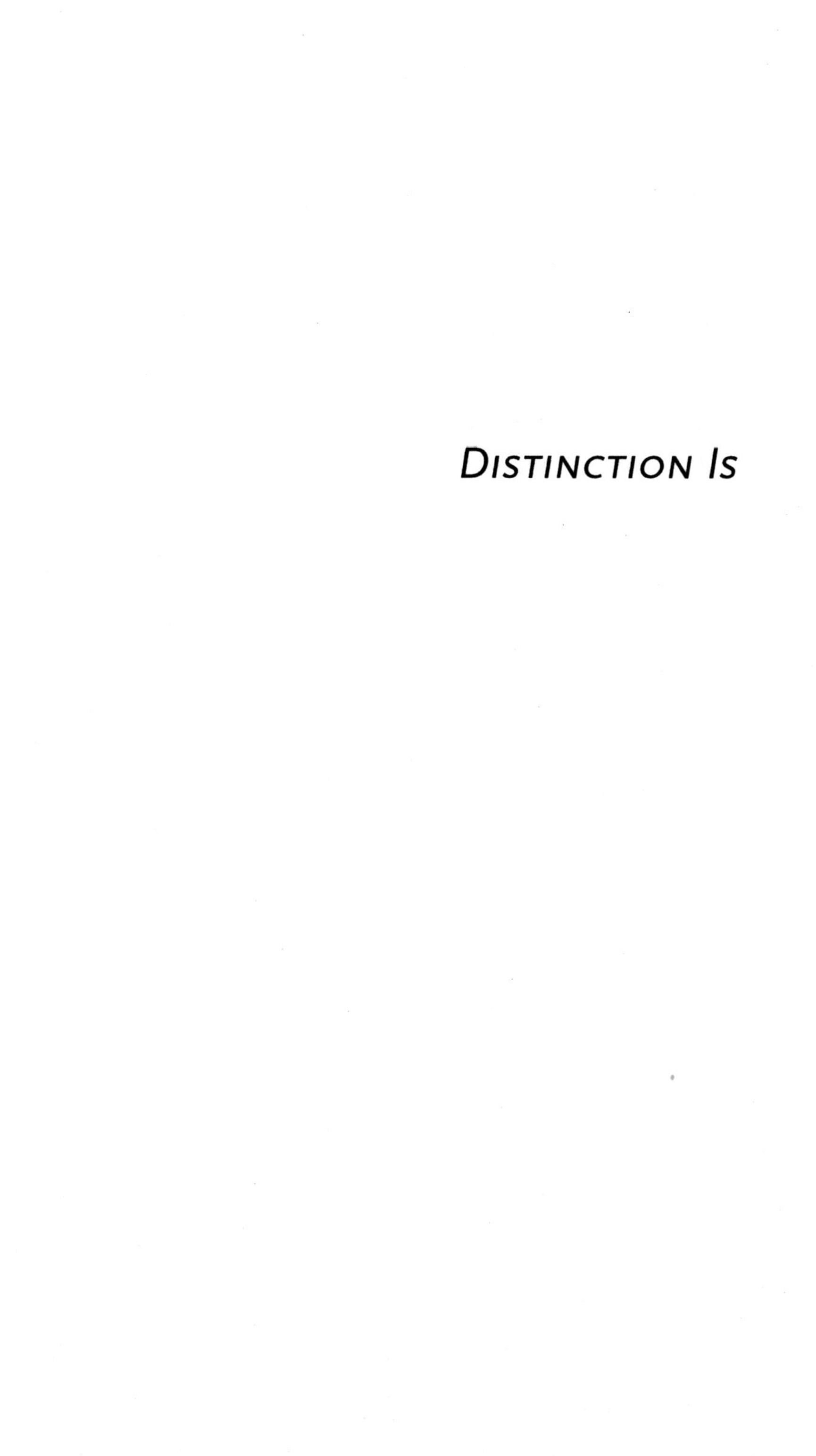

Distinction Is

This work that
smoke could it
be I have nothing

I want O just
to write it once
I am good like

a chocolate or a
painting someone
honest couldn't

lie I lie not
once to please
please lie tell

something to me
a star is a star
distinction is

exhaust fills
the air several
birds cry spring

it is not are
we somewhere
we are not

be here
be here the
bus comes

loaded no child-
ren later sirens
explode a life

gone terrorism
happens there
no conclusions

NOT/INSPIRATION BUT TRAFFIC

In Vermont
the days go
greyly on

apart from the
occasional passing
jet & hum

of the refrigerator
the only sound
is fire's hiss

a serpent in
the midst
with no thought

pure action
must come from
some instigation

the struck match
bellows breath
my thought

that something
should burn

The air crisp OPEC
corrupt this day
began like the
others with light
the IMF
indentures people
to implacable
shacks built on
the hillside
why do we
not take inspiration
from this bullshit
wind & cut
the strata
that presses us
or pierce it
like a steeple
does the sky
all holy & self-
righteously excused
the wind is my
least favorite
of the elements
just as credit is my
least favorite abstraction

The light grows long
as the year works
through the brick

where shadows
eclipse the
new slats on

the fence it has
been months
since I dreamed

of leaving what
came of me
while here

the trip to
the auto parts
store to fix

the tail light
broken on the car
light fading as

I stood & talked
to a friend I
didn't know

was a friend
have I respected
them all at least

as much as they
respected me

Work, kindly let me be
who or what I am I do

out the window
the evening I drink

call it what you
will I am broke

snow falls
thought's curtain

I said no deal
you can't sell

this workday to me
mostly wasted

time this
task too much

I'll miss the
system here

I hope as I'm
leaving my message

is clear not fucked
up functioning like

a foolhardy wheel

The wind blows not
inspiration but traffic
mid-May I just got

paid pollen a submarine
no longer submerged
a crowd on the corner

a child on a swing
a man runs shirtless
in the breeze my throat

chokes I am about
to see a friend

Everyone will always be moving through the fevered grass
we are not who we were   who we are

are people in love in panic in love with memory
fish who croak enfranchise our songs

disinherited by other bodies you send me the years
in envelopes posted with questions did you

really oh I heard it from someone no
I didn't yes I did really

Window faces
trees grass fern

light when we
have it blooms

inside dew
laden grass

dandelions cold
unopen sway

over moth
shadow ground

red flags left
by utility men

perhaps to mark
distance between

what is useful &
not meant for us

After Breathing It In

This is Providence.
I am leaving it
where it is.

What's left of
the stars still
burns. A jet passes.

My friends are
where they are.

Love grows languid.

A horse with a
bunch of birds
on its back

The city a class in light moves a train
through a tunnel. Fear of beauty
is the fear to speak unknown names
in sleep. Wake up a light a city in which

you walk. Breath rots. Breath forgets
where it was & becomes yours to
forget who was cruel to it by breathing
it out after breathing it in.

Yes, it's a city
there are boys
who sit women
who walk parking
lots abandoned
traffic spare
tires gardens

Yes, this could be
a town it's a city
whose history is
the sky grows large
the trees grow large
the sun burns
the wall

Clearly no
commitment
from either
hand either
to hold or to
write Philly
is no joke
the couples at
the dark manor
drink Olde
English with
straws gripping
their lips
one hand
committed to
grasp the
can the other
to gesture loss:
I gave you
a 10 you
gave me a
dollar back:
I'm gonnna
kick their
fuckin' ass

WINDOWS WE

To begin where I left
off is to begin where I will
never be again. The house.

Look. We walked through
a door. The door moved.
A boy. A mother.

Windows filled with light.
Not there I am
awake. The light.

Foundation. My family
Caroline. Foundation.
I should give.

I have refused the house.
It lives. My mouth
its door. My eyes.

The moon stricken
from Monday's events
meant the sun would
hang half-heartedly

in my eye   Neanderthals
reveal their history
in crude art or
maybe it's no art

at all   If they could
see how we
depict them would
they continue to

depict themselves
big headed & obedient
to some strange design
This poem began with

the disappearance of the
moon only to ask what do
Neanderthals have to do
with anything anyway

My eyes tiny
squids smashed
into the light

Reading again
Berrigan &
Ceravolo

The rain like
Caroline watches
from the bridge

Baroque gone the
way of all breath

we try to say
things are what

they are material
is material a sign

to read is dangerous
for we may read

too deeply & find
the fissure or

we may either find
the angel or the person

better to us than
the other material is

material & things are
often what they are

Zeitgeist
in the grocer's
sign nothing

seems to happen
something happens
leaves burn

face the sun
no measure to
sky   window

the president
meets the house
speaker   whose

safe   whose
a friend enough
not to be

fired Alberto
Gonzalez
is that friend

zeitgeist takes
more than one
               always

go   it's
the 1970s
right now

wires over
Telegraph
wires over

Walnut or
Chelten &
Pulaski   a

place no one
knows   broke
        teach commitment

        teach commitment
rain falls   an award
released the piano

hangs around the bass
give a reason why
writing is significant

if writing only happens
when the world is tired
the piano the grand

piano is not through
walking & talking
Al Greer on drums

some voice over it
all voice need not be
found voice is

release voice from
commitment let it
play   noise

call it music call
the rhino in the dream
a buck in reality

            a roll
   a tribute   this
is okay

        non-negotiable
cold the color cold
everyday for years

thank you
a job   to do
what   an American

should it be this
hard to suck
                tired

morning
            morning
                    morning

try & do that he
says   snow about
his neck   a lace

how to
write
any of it

            rain
run in rain run in
            rain

rhythm radio
rhythm radio
    squandered

what have you done
I have done
interregnum

dishes in a xylophone
sink   drum fill
no lead

just do time
the rest have
done time

the bills add
up when nothing
else does

what's new
this leaks as
does that

no NSA
agitprop necessary
a leak is a leak

the beat is the
beat we face
burning in the eye

a burning
hell ready
or not

you're it   why
do we have stars
when we can't feel

the light in
the grocer's sign
the 'h' in 'the'

burnt out trapped
in non-light
crisp green cabeza

crisp green cabbage
3 for 88 cents
a deal w/o a piano

solo the earth is
frightening
to say we're getting

fucked w/o saying
we're getting fucked
impossible saying

this when getting
& having are much
the same

a broadcast service
Philadelphia
now in HD

wish   a place
to walk to   a star
in sight   a friend

to talk to kind
of lonesome tonight
it's getting colder

wish the moon
would give some
light how to wish

this song would end
            this song
  doesn't end

somebody else
on the horns
tonight the alarm

the same aahng
aahng aahng
aahng aahng

it's the horn
holds together
the cart crash

bang across the way
exhaustion pushes
the envelope

Lee Morgan & Paul
Chambers   love
          sleep

so the drummer
makes
possible

possibility
the whistle
listen

no trio to
obey no quartet
the voice

misunderstood
cadence
marriage

the back
beat that
keeps it

zeitgeist
zeit for ____
geist for ____

Bush says
lessons for
Iraq in Vietnam

we plastic we
windows we
storm we

don't need
to fast-forward
it's all here

each step
as significant
as toothpaste

nothing
dark
coming
to
life
the
street
is
either
this
or
that
perspective
on
the
park
not
further
from
here
the
laundromat
is
the
same
brick
is
brick
the
section
of
the
street
I
didn't
know
it
was
raining
it
was
dark

it
is
big
&
small

            & why shouldn't we be
warmer   the earth as it
is needs another

rage
              the mind burns
eyelids   with

constancy   not leaning
any direction   more
a tangle than a tie

WHERE HOUSES REMAINED

idle. fickle. no crowd
commits to any truth
beyond the one manifest

before them. a bridge.
a river skyline reflects
in. to make place one

must place it in mem-
ory so that each
day it is there. present.

dctritus alleviates respons-
ibility. takes place away
like paint poorly

laid upon canvas. order
sets its own table.
considers its dishes.

makes memory enlist
whole hock in the house-
hold's hives. conviction

is conviction. acts
not as one should.
acts as one does.

I see through glass

                                       as it

      is

                rock

                    made sonic

clear

      it breaks

                no hearts

      it breaks

          step

            with

its past

       the digital

            is

         no break

                  whole dots

                          cipher

a skein

      in a manner

               derived

        from some past

you hear

my voice

objectivity

sets in

voice is no

object

to render the aorta

is not the heart

you mean

nor is it the heart

I meant

someone to

have

like glass

it remained but broke

as I tried to see

through its stages

of rock

your voice makes

my hands

feel heart

through my skin

the ego

a weird window

through

which

we   see

as if voices through
a hall I am aware
the birds' relevancy
completes biology's steps

grief   ruby   sapphire
the stones project
an awful radiance made
true by faults

chill bones frame a still
warm heart   you see
the tree names
according to what it was

once it held us
we became angry
with confrontation
like smoke the feeling

faded like sound it
reverberated in the ear
& boy did bird swing
in the evening time

where I moved was
absolutely not based
on belief but a story
where houses remained

the dozen or so miles
my stomach swelled
with seeds didn't last
long enough for any of us

light I may have said turned
phlegmatic in the eye don't
take this to be rerun at
night take it to run

display the crystals
in the body goliath

stricken with insomnia
puked blood because

blood was blue & made
sense now sense can be
made what it was
grief a lukewarm

heart surrounded by
cold sinew once
used for string so
that song could exist

should a canary consider
itself lucky if it could
still shadow against the
branches relevant &

not so boring in its flight

B/W SONG & GLASS

The domestic scene
                    a room

    6:57   Caroline
        sleeps the fan

above her   spins married
two years we have

moved   changed
I am not the man

I was   real is
real   love   love

more than the vow
            b/w song & glass

Acknowledgments

Thanks to the following editors for publishing portions of this book
in their journals: Tony Tost at *Fascicle*, Chris & Jenn McCreary at
Ixnay, & Jonathan Minton at *word for/word*.

For advice during the writing and editing of this book, thanks to
Carolina Maugeri, Michael Gizzi, Brandon Som, Scott Bryan Wilson,
Eli Goldblatt, Dan Featherston, Noah Eli Gordon, & Elisabeth
Sheffield & her students in the Publishing Workshop. For shelter in
the summer of 2006, I thank Michael & Pamela Hayes.

"The din comes as sun" after Martin Johnston & Rodney Koencke

"Forever dedicated to the" after MC Offwhyte & Maker

"The light grows long" for Xue Di & Ben Sherman who live in
New England

"Work, kindly let me be" after Townes Van Zandt

"The wind blows not" for Jason Ajemian

"Everyone will always be moving through the fevered grass" for
Jason Ajemian

"as if voices through" after Andy Chase

"The domestic scene" for Caroline